Cockney
Rhyming
Slang

NEED
A SMASH
AND GRAB?

Shelley Klein

Cockney Rhyming Slang

NEED
A SMASH
AND GRAB?

Michael O'Mara Books Limited

First published in Great Britain in 2009 by
Michael O'Mara Books Limited
9 Lion Yard
Tremadoc Road
London SW4 7NQ

A CIP catalogue record for this book is available from the British Library.

Papers used by Michael O'Mara Books Limited are natural, recyclable products made from
wood grown in sustainable forests. The manufacturing processes conform to the
environmental regulations of the country of origin.

ISBN: 978-1-84317-374-8

5 6 7 8 9 10

www.mombooks.com

Designed and typeset by Glen Saville

Printed and bound by Estella Print, Spain

INTRODUCTION

If you were to visit the East End of London you might well come across a street trader offering you some 'early hours' or 'Gertie Gitanas' and you wouldn't be alone in feeling puzzled. After all Cockney rhyming slang was originally invented for just this purpose i.e. the complete bamboozlement of those not in the know. Yet it has survived into the 21st century because it is constantly being updated with new and wonderfully expressive phrases. It's a living language, a fun, easy-to-pick-up secret patois that has extremely old roots – some of which date as far back as the eighteenth century.

However, if it hadn't been for various people documenting these and all the other pieces of Cockney rhyming slang over the years we might never have been fortunate enough to know about them. For this we have to thank people such as Henry Mayhew who wrote *London Labour and the London Poor* in 1851 and who observed, 'The new style of cadgers [street traders] cant is done all on the rhyming principle'; John Camden Hotten's *The Slang Dictionary* which was published in 1859 and the pseudonymous Ducange Anglicus's *The*

Vulgar Tongue published in 1857. Without them and a whole host of others, contemporary rhyming slang would be all the poorer and the pages of this book all the shorter.

This little collection does not pretend to be a definitive study of this wayward language; rather it is a straightforward guide to some of the most frequently used, up-to-date as well as old-fashioned phrases. It is easy to follow and gives brief explanations to all the phrases included, although frequently, when employing Cockney rhyming slang, the whole phrase is often shortened to just one word, for example 'Barnet Fair' meaning 'hair' is often shortened to 'barnet', as in 'I can't do anything with my barnet this morning, it's all over the place!'

So, as they say up the East End, put your plates of meat up, pour yourself a Britney and enjoy!

COCKNEY TO ENGLISH

Abergavenny = a penny
'I don't have an Abergavenny!'
Given that Cockney rhyming slang was the argot of street vendors it is not surprising that there are several words and phrases to describe money (see also 'bread and honey'). A small Welsh town, Abergavenny is a perfect rhyme for a 'penny'.

Adam and Eve = believe
'Would you Adam and Eve it!'
A popular phrase from the mid-nineteenth century, 'I don't Adam and Eve it' is still in use today to express disbelief.

airs and graces = braces
'Mother, where have you put me airs and graces?'
Clothing features highly in Cockney rhyming slang and some of the longest surviving phrases allude to the type of clothing that was most popular in the nineteenth and early twentieth century such as waistcoats, spats, collars and braces. Other Cockney words for braces are 'Epsom races' and 'Ascot races', which was normally abbreviated to the much snappier 'Ascots'.

almond rocks = socks

'There's a hole in me almonds.'

A lovely-sounding rhyme which is often shortened simply to 'almonds'. It is believed that almond rocks were a popular sweetmeat in the Victorian period.

Anna Maria = fire

'Throw some more coal on the Anna Maria.'

Dating from the nineteenth century, 'Anna Maria' (pronounced 'Mer-eye-er') refers to a fire in a grate rather than a house on fire. Variations include 'Ave Maria'.

Anneka Rice = advice

'I could do with some Anneka Rice, mate.'

Best known for the TV programme *Challenge Anneka*, Anneka Rice became a well-known TV personality in the 1980s and 90s, which is no doubt why her name was adopted by Cockney rhyming slang to mean 'advice'.

apple fritter = bitter/beer

'Pint of apple fritter please.'

A very popular drink in London – ordering an 'apple' is a well-established phrase.

apple pips (also see 'battleships') = lips
'Give us a kiss on me apples?'
Thought to have originated in the early part of the twentieth century – this phrase is usually shortened to 'apples'.

apples and pears = stairs
'Let's go up the apple and pears to Uncle Ned.'
Probably the best-known of all Cockney phrases, 'apples and pears' was first recorded in the mid-1850s and is still in use today. Here, however, is an example from *Sinister Street* by Compton Mackenzie (1914):
>   'I soon shoved him down the apples and pears.'
>   'I haven't understood a word of that last sentence,' said Michael.
>   'Don't you know back slang-slang and rhyming slang? Oh, it's grand!'

April fools = tools
'Pass me April fools – I need to fix the cupboard.'
Coined in the Victorian period and initially referring only to the kind of tools needed to burgle a house, these days 'April fools' can be applied to any tools in the box.

Aristotle = bottle
'Pass the Arry, me lad.'
Named after the Greek philosopher, this piece of slang is frequently shortened to 'Arry'.

army and navy = gravy
'This meat needs more army.'
Dating from around World War I, 'army and navy' was used a lot by members of the armed services, probably because gravy was in abundance in the canteens.

artful dodger = lodger
'I need an artful dodger for the spare room.'
Charles Dickens, who wrote *Oliver Twist* in 1838, might be the one responsible for this piece of rhyming slang, which was first recorded in use circa 1859. However, owing to the bad reputation of lodgers in general for sneaking away without paying their rent, the use of the phrase 'artful dodger' for a lodger might just be a coincidence.

Auntie Ella = umbrella
'Get out the Auntie Ella, it's chucking it down.'
Given Britain's inclement weather it is little wonder Cockney rhyming slang has a word for an umbrella. Originally 'Isabella' was favoured but later this changed to an 'Auntie Ella', a phrase still current today.

Auntie Nellie = belly
'Oh, me Auntie Nellie's killing me!'
Whoever the original Auntie Nellie was, I can't imagine that she would have been hugely flattered to have her name doubled up to mean belly.

Nevertheless this phrase was and still is frequently used to denote the stomach and, in particular, one that is upset.

B

babbling brook = crook (or sometimes cook)
'You're a real babbling brook.'
Because Cockney rhyming slang was the language of London's streets and markets, several phrases appear in its lexicon for crooks and thieves, this one being popular from the early 1920s onwards. See also 'tea leaf'.

ball of chalk = walk
'I'm going for a ball of chalk.'
This is the most popular rhyme for 'walk', although several others exist, nearly all of them using 'chalk', such as 'powdered chalk' and 'penn'orth [a penny's worth] of chalk'.

ball of fat = cat

'Put some milk out for the ball of fat.'

A wonderfully descriptive phrase that sums up just what happens when you overfeed your pet! Variants include 'this and that'.

Barnaby Rudge = judge

'He's up in front of the Barnaby tomorrow.'

The title of one of Charles Dickens's many novels, *Barnaby Rudge* was published in 1841 so might well be the origin of this phrase for a 'judge', given that one of the book's themes is capital punishment.

Barney Rubble = trouble

'Don't get into any Barney.'

No doubt based upon the long-standing 'barney' meaning a fight – 'Barney Rubble' is taken from the cartoon character of the same name in *The Flintstones*.

Barnet Fair = hair

'Get your barnet sorted.'

An enduring and much-loved rhyme, which is now almost always shortened simply to, 'barnet', as the following example from Frank Norman's book *The Guntz* illustrates well: 'They send you to a doss house, so that you can get lice in your barnet.'

bat and wicket = ticket

'I haven't bought a bat and wicket.'

Most often applied to tickets for travelling, i.e. train tickets, this piece of slang uses a cricket analogy.

battleships (also see 'apple pips') = lips

'Stop licking your battles.'

'Battleships' and 'apple pips' are the two oldest and most common phrases for 'lips'.

bear's paw = saw (tool)

'Pass the bear's, would you, lad?'

Coined in the nineteenth century, this rhyming slang does not seem to be associated with one trade in particular but is a general word for a 'saw'.

beggar-my-neighbour = the labour (exchange)/being on the dole

'I'm off down the beggar.'

Usually shortened to 'beggar' – being 'on the beggar' simply means being out of work, not begging (though that could be a feared consequence). A labour exchange is now called a job centre.

belt and braces = races
'I'm going to have a bet on the belts.'
Horseracing being one of the most popular pastimes in the nineteenth century, it is little wonder that a piece of slang was invented for it.

Ben Flake = steak
'I fancy a nice juicy Ben Flake.'
First recorded in use circa 1859, this phrase is not currently heard a great deal, having been replaced with the more popular 'Joe Blake'.

Bessie Braddock = haddock
'Fancy some chips with your Bessie?'
Named after a former member of parliament who was rather overweight, suggesting she might have enjoyed too many fish suppers, this term was very popular in the 1950s and 60s.

Bexleyheath (also see Hampstead Heath) = teeth
'Put your Bexleys in, Dad!'
Bexleyheath in south-east London and Hampstead Heath in North London were both used in the latter part of the nineteenth century as rhyming slang for teeth – the phrases being shortened to either
Bexleys or Hampsteads.

Billy Button = mutton

'I can't wait to get my teeth into this Billy.'

Since mutton is no longer as popular, the term 'Billy Button' is not heard as often as it was in the Victorian era, but is nonetheless still current.

birdlime = time

'He's been doing birdlime in Holloway.'

Normally referring to 'time served in prison', i.e. a prison sentence, 'birdlime' is particularly apt as it is a substance used to trap birds.

biscuits and cheese = knees

'Me biscuits and cheese were knocking together.'

Not one of the oldest pieces of rhyming slang; nonetheless this phrase, dating from the 1940s, is often shortened to 'biscuits' for easier use, as in 'My biscuits are hurting me.'

black and white = night

'This street's dangerous on a dark black and white.'

Both this phrase and variant 'take a fright' seem very apt descriptions.

Bo Peep = sheep

'Can you see the Bo Peep in that field?'

Early-twentieth century in origin and taken from the nursery rhyme 'Little Bo Peep', this phrase is normally used when speaking to children.

boat and oar = whore (prostitute)

'This street's full of boat and oars.'

Coined in the mid-twentieth century, this term was later replaced by others such as 'bolt the door' or 'Jane Shore', after Edward VI's mistress.

Boat Race = face

'You've a lovely boat race.'

One of the most popular pieces of rhyming slang, which often crops up in its shorter form, i.e. 'boat', in various British TV programmes in order to bestow genuine Cockney charm on a character. The phrase has been linked to the Oxford and Cambridge Boat Race which has taken place every year on the Thames since 1829.

Bob Squash = wash

'You'll be needing a bob after the football.'

Having a 'bob' is still a popular piece of slang for washing oneself, however 'a bob' can also refer to a bathroom or washroom.

borrow and beg = egg
'Half a dozen borrows, please.'
Dating from a time when eggs weren't available on demand, the phrase 'borrow and beg' perhaps refers to the lengths people would go to to lay their hands on one!

bow and arrow = sparrow
'Look at all those bow and arrows.'
A nineteenth-century term for that once most common of all London birds, save the pigeon.

bowl the hoop = soup
'Do you want some bread with your bowl the hoop?'
This slang refers to the popular Victorian children's game of bowling a metal hoop along the streets and seeing how long one could keep it going.

bowler hat = rat
'I just saw a bowler in the kitchen.'
They say that in London you are never very far away from a rodent. Other Cockney phrases for 'rat' include 'cocked hat'.

Brad Pitts = breasts (tits)
'Check out the Brad Pitts on her!'
Rhyming with the word 'tit', the name of the Hollywood actor Brad Pitt forms the perfect slang for breasts. On occasion the rhyme is changed to 'bradleys'.

bread and butter = gutter
'He's in the butter again.'
As plenty of Londoners lived fairly impoverished lives, there are many phrases that refer to money or its lack.

bread and honey = money
'We haven't enough bread to pay the rent.'
Probably brought to our shores by the Americans, 'bread', meaning money, was adopted into rhyming slang.

brewer's bung = tongue
'Hold your brewer's, I'm talking.'
Another reference to drinking culture, this phrase is often shortened.

Britney Spears = beers
'Let's have a few Britneys.'
One of the most recent additions to the Cockney lexicon, 'having a Britney' obviously refers to the American pop icon Britney Spears, and is today the most popular rhyme for a beer.

Brussels sprouts = Scouts

'He's away at camp with the Brussels.'

Boy Scouts were given this rhyme, which is often shortened.

bubble bath = laugh

'He's having a bubble bath.'

Still commonly used, other expressions for laugh include 'giraffe' and 'Steffi Graf', who was a many-times Wimbledon champion.

bubbly jock = turkey

'Let's have a bubbly for Christmas dinner.'

A 'turkey cock' is the basis for this piece of nineteenth-century slang – perhaps coined because of the funny, gobbling sound turkeys often make.

bucket and pail = jail

'He'll end up in the bucket if he carries on like this.'

Apt given the buckets used in jails for drinking water and the pails used to urinate in, this rhyming slang sums up the poor conditions inside a prison in the nineteenth century.

bull and cow = row (quarrel)

'They're having a bull and cow in the kitchen.'

This is thought to be a very old piece of Cockney rhyming slang, although it wasn't recorded until 1859.

Burton-on-Trent = rent
'You'd better have the Burton by Monday.'
Nineteenth century in origin, 'Burton-on-Trent' is sometimes replaced by the less popular 'Duke of Kent'.

bushel and peck = neck
'He's a right pain in the bushel.'
Coined in the later part of the nineteenth century and usually shortened. Other phrases for 'neck' include 'Gregory Peck'.

Bushey Park = lark (joke)
'You're having a bushey!'
Having a bit of a lark sounds rather old-fashioned these days, but back in Victorian times this phrase, named after the parkland to the north of Hampton Court Palace, was often heard.

butcher's hook = a look
'Let's have a good butcher's then.'
One of the few pieces of Cockney rhyming slang which, in its shortened form, i.e. 'butcher's', has now established itself in general popular slang.

Cain and Abel = table
'We're having tea at the Cain and Abel.'
First recorded in usage circa 1859 this phrase is one of the oldest in
Cockney rhyming history.

Calvin Klein = fine
'You are looking damn Calvin today!'
The American designer Calvin Klein is the unwitting progenitor of this
piece of slang meaning to look fine or fit, i.e. in good physical form!

Camilla Parker Bowles = Rolls (Rolls-Royce)
'Let's go in the Camilla today, Charles.'
A 'Camilla Parker Bowles' meaning a Rolls-Royce is a very recent addition
to rhyming slang – and obviously takes as its source Prince Charles's
second wife. This phrase is often shortened to 'Camilla' or even 'Camilla
Parker'.

Captain Cook = book
'You have to read this captain.'
Although this rhyme was originally coined for books in general, at some

point it came to be more specifically linked to horseracing and bookies. The rhyme refers to Captain James Cook (1728-1779) who claimed to have 'discovered' Australia while sailing on HMS *Endeavour*.

carving knife = wife
'Where's your carving this evening?'
Not as frequently used as the more popular 'trouble and strife' meaning wife, 'carving knife' was hopefully created because of the domestic association of knives with kitchens and women rather than the more sinister cutting qualities of said instruments!

cat and mouse = a house
'We've put the cat and mouse up for sale.'
Mice were a huge problem during the Victorian period – most houses containing at least one or two of the pesky little rodents. The solution was to keep a household cat, hence this piece of rhyming slang. See also 'Mickey mouse'.

Charlie Dicken = chicken
'That was a lovely Charlie we ate last night.'
Named after the famous nineteenth-century novelist, Charles Dickens. John Ayto notes in his *Dictionary of Rhyming Slang* that chicken was not such a popular food item as it is these days, with most people in the nineteenth century keeping chickens for their eggs rather than their meat.

cheerful giver = liver

'Me cheerful giver's not going to thank me tomorrow.'

An early-to-mid-twentieth-century phrase; variants include 'bow and quiver'.

cherry hog = dog

'Let's have a flutter down the cherries.'

In nineteenth-century London, cherry stones were often referred to as hogs – hence this particular rhyme meaning a dog. A good night out 'down the cherries' meant a good night out at the dog track.

cherry ripe = pipe/tripe

'I'm going to sit by the fire with me cherry ripe.'

More frequently used to refer to a pipe, the phrase was coined in the nineteenth century when pipes were quite often made of cherry wood. However it also denotes 'tripe' meaning utter nonsense, rather than the lining of a sheep's stomach.

china plate = mate

'How y'doing, me old china?'

Most frequently used in its shortened form – the longer version 'china plate' was first recorded in the 1880s.

cock linnet = minute

'Wait a cock linnet, would you?'

Mentioned in the famous music-hall song of 1919 'Don't Dilly-Dally on the Way', it was inevitable that a cock linnet would find its way into the Cockney lexicon, particularly since 'minute' is hard to find a rhyme for.

cock sparrow = barrow

'Get the fish out the cock sparrow, me lad.'

According to Julian Franklyn in his marvellously comprehensive study of Cockney, *A Dictionary of Rhyming Slang*, this phrase is still current among East End market traders, particularly the costermongers.

cockroach = coach

'We're all going on the cockroach to Brighton.'

Not the oldest piece of Cockney rhyming slang, it is thought that the phrase was first coined after World War II when a lot of Londoners started taking coach trips to the seaside in an attempt to cheer themselves up.

Conan Doyle = boil

'I've got a Conan Doyle on me back.'

Taken from the name of the creator of Sherlock Holmes, this rather unflattering rhyme can still be heard to describe this nasty complaint.

corns and bunions = onions
'I'll take a bag of corns and bunions.'
Used by costermongers, 'corns and bunions' is still a phrase heard today.

cream crackered = knackered (tired)
'I'm cream crackered'
An extremely popular piece of slang to express feeling exhausted (knackered). Can also mean 'broken', as in 'my car's cream crackered'.

currant bun = son/the sun
'May I introduce you to my currant bun'
Variations on this theme are 'custard bun', 'Bath bun' and 'hot cross bun.'

cut and carried = married
'I'm getting cut in the morning.'
One of the oldest Cockney phrases for the state of being married, 'cut and carried' refers to an agricultural term for the cutting and carrying of corn back to the barns at harvest time.

cuts and scratches = matches
'Give us a lend of your cuts and scratches.'
The onomatopoeic potential of the word 'scratches' (being the sound a match makes when drawn across sandpaper) has obviously influenced this piece of rhyming slang.

daffadown dilly (or 'daffadowndilly') = silly
'Don't be so daffadown dilly.'
Probably referring to the nineteenth century 'daffy', meaning 'daft',
and combining this with another nineteenth-century piece of slang,
'dilly', meaning 'foolish', 'daffadown dilly' is a popular if slightly odd
piece of slang.

Daily Mail = tale
'He's telling Daily Mails again.'
Believed to have first been coined in the 1930s, this rhyming slang
might well have expressed the incredulity of the public towards Britain's
tabloid press.

daisy roots = boots
'You'll be needing some sturdy daisies in this weather.'
A very popular piece of rhyming slang that was first recorded in 1859.
It also appears in the Lonnie Donegan song 'My Old Man's a Dustman': '...
He's got such a job to pull them up that he calls them daisy roots.'

Davina McCalls = balls

'She kicked me in the Davinas!'

Taken from the name of the popular TV host, 'Davina McCalls' is now a very common piece of rhyming slang for that most sensitive part of the male anatomy.

dickory dock = clock

'We're late! Look at the dickory dock!'

No doubt coined from the nursery rhyme 'Hickory Dickory Dock', this rhyme was common parlance in the nineteenth century.

dicky bird = word

'I give you my dicky bird I didn't do it!'

Originally referring to the swearing of an oath, 'dicky bird' has now become more general in meaning.

Dicky Dirt = shirt

'Can you iron me dicky, please?'

Still in use today in its shortened form, this rhyme was one of the earliest in the lexicon, dating from the 1800s.

dig a grave = shave

'He was at the mirror digging his chin.'

Apparently Australian in origin but quickly adopted by the British, this phrase was first coined in the early part of the twentieth century and is frequently shortened to 'dig'.

ding-dong = song
'Give us a ding-dong.'
First recorded in the mid 1900s, having a bit of a ding-dong still survives as a phrase today.

Doctor Crippen = dripping
'I'll have some Doctor Crippen on me bread.'
Doctor Hawley Harvey Crippen must be one of Britain's most notorious murderers which makes this piece of rhyming slang a little sinister – particularly when one considers that dripping is the congealed fat from a piece of roast meat.

dog and bone = phone
'Get on the dog and tell him to get over here now.'
Not a particularly old piece of rhyming slang, nevertheless this is one of the most popular phrases – and is still in common use today.

Doris Day = gay
'He's definitely Doris Day.'
Using the name of the American singer and actress, this is mid-twentieth century in origin.

drum and fife = knife

'Watch out, he's got a drum in his pocket.'

Dating from the nineteenth century, 'drum and fife' obviously has military connotations. Other Cockney phrases for a knife include 'husband and wife', which is often shortened to 'husband'.

E

early hours = flowers

'What beautiful early hours.'

Given that traders at the main flower market (which used to be located in Covent Garden, central London) had to get up very early to do business, this piece of Cockney rhyming slang should be self-explanatory.

earwig = understand (twig)

'I've only just earwigged what you mean.'

To 'twig' is in itself a slang word meaning to understand – hence the rhyme to 'earwig' – which can also mean to overhear something you shouldn't, i.e. 'stop your earwigging'.

Eddie Grundies = undies (underwear)

A popular rhyme for underwear, 'Eddie Grundies' takes as its source the kindly rogue of the same name who appears in BBC Radio 4's long-running soap opera, *The Archers*.

eighteen pence = sense

'Ain't you got no bleedin' eighteen pence?'

First recorded in the mid-nineteenth century and still occasionally heard today.

elephant's trunk = drunk

'He's elephant's!'

This was first recorded in use in 1859 and is still current today.

Farmer Giles = haemorrhoids (piles)

'Me farmers are giving me grief today.'

One of the earliest pieces of Cockney rhyming slang, 'Farmer Giles' comes from the eighteenth century. Other phrases to describe this most awkward of complaints are 'Chalfont St Giles' and 'Nuremberg Trials', often shortened to 'Nurembergs'.

field of wheat = street
'I'm taking a walk down the old field of wheat.'
Given that the streets of London – particularly back in the nineteenth century – were as far from fields of wheat as possible (i.e. they were smog-ridden, sooty, dangerous places) one can only assume that this particular rhyme was begun with tongue firmly planted in cheek!

fife and drum = bum
'Does my fife look big in this?'
A late-nineteenth-century rhyme – probably begun because both drums and bums get beaten!

fine and dandy = brandy
'Pour me a drop of fine and dandy.'
Pub life being very important to the London working man, particularly in the nineteenth century, there are several terms for brandy, including, from the twentieth century, 'Mahatma Ghandi'.

fisherman's daughter = water

'Get me a glass of fisherman's.'

Used generally by fish merchants and those involved in the fishing industry, 'fisherman's daughter' most often refers to drinking water as opposed to large volumes of water like seas or oceans.

fleas and ants = pants

'There's a hole in me fleas.'

This piece of slang probably originated in the 1930s and although current today is not frequently used.

flowery dell = cell

'Stick him in the flowery.'

Coined no doubt with tongue firmly planted in cheek given that a prison cell is hardly going to be full of flowers. This phrase is often shortened to 'flowers' or 'flowery'.

frog and toad = road

'Keep off the frog and toad.'

A mid-nineteenth-century phrase, which is still current today and which might have begun because frogs and toads tend to get driven over or trodden upon when they venture onto Britain's roads.

garden gate = magistrate/mate
'He's up before the garden gate tomorrow.'
Still occasionally used today this piece of rhyming slang was first recorded in use circa 1859.

garden plant = aunt
'I'm going round my garden's for a cup of tea.'
A twentieth-century rhyme which is usually shortened.

gay and frisky = whisky
'I'm dying for a gay and frisky.'
A very popular piece of rhyming slang thought to have originated in the 1920s.

Geoff Hurst = first (as in a first-class degree)
'I got a Geoff Hurst in my exams!'
Not only does 'Hurst' rhyme perfectly with 'first' but Sir Geoffrey Hurst was definitely a first among English footballers as it was he who scored a hat-trick for England against West Germany in the 1966 World Cup.

Gertie Gitana = banana

'Gertie Gitana', referring to a twentieth-century music-hall act, was a very popular phrase in the Victorian period.

giggle and titter = bitter (i.e. beer)

'Let's go down the pub for a giggle.'

A very fitting piece of slang summing up perfectly the effect a couple of beers can have on the drinker!

ginger beer = queer (homosexual)

'I reckon he's a ginger.'

Used almost exclusively within the ranks of the Merchant Navy and around the docks, this phrase, which originates from the 1920s, was often shortened to 'ginger'.

give and take = cake

'Have a slice of give and take.'

Not quite so popular these days, this phrase originates in the nineteenth century.

Glasgow Rangers (also see Queen's Park Rangers) = strangers

'Watch out! There's a lot of Glasgows around here.'

Named after the Scottish football club, 'Glasgow Rangers' is often shortened to 'Glasgows'. According to one authority on the subject this phrase was most often used amongst the criminal fraternity – most especially street look-outs on the watch for the police.

God forbids = kids
'Got to get home to the god forbids.'
Popular from the beginning of the nineteenth century onwards, other phrases for 'kids' include 'dustbin lids' and 'saucepan lids'.

goose's neck = cheque
'I'll write you a goose's'
Frequently shortened to 'goose's' this piece of rhyming slang (alongside chicken's neck) is still in use today, though with the number of cheques issued dwindling fast, it might soon fall out of usage.

grasshopper = copper
'Look out, the grasshoppers are coming!'
Referring not only to policemen but also to their informants (i.e. grasses) this phrase is late nineteenth century in origin but is still heard frequently today – particularly on TV dramas about cops and robbers such as *The Bill*.

greengages = wages
'I'm off to pick up me greens.'
An early-twentieth-century phrase most often reduced simply to 'greens'.

half-inch = pinch (steal)
'He's half-inched my handbag!'
Variously described as being a mid-nineteenth-century phrase as well as
one coined in the 1920s, 'half-inch' is still in use today.

halfpenny dip = ship
'There's a halfpenny on the horizon.'
Coined by dockers in the mid-nineteenth century, this phrase is still
functional today but is not to be confused with 'old whip', which usually
refers to a ship that a seaman is serving on.

Hampstead Heath (also see Bexleyheath) = teeth
'Better put me hampsteads in.'
Coined in the mid-nineteenth century this piece of rhyming slang still
enjoys popularity today.

Hansel and Gretel = kettle
'Put the Hansel on, I'm thirsty.'
Named after the children's fairy-tale characters and normally shortened
to 'Hansel'.

Harry Randall = candle/handle

'Light the Harrys, will you, mother?'

Harry Randall was an early-twentieth-century comedian but what he had to do with candles is anyone's guess. Later, the term was adapted to include 'handle', as in 'the Harry on this door is stuck.'

Harvey Nichols = pickles

'Where have you put that jar of Harveys?'

Harvey Nichols, the up-market designer food and clothing store in Knightsbridge, London, seems an unlikely rhyme for 'pickles', nevertheless a jar of 'Harveys' is a commonplace rhyme – probably conceived with a hint of irony.

hearts of oak = broke (penniless)

'He lost his job and now he's hearts.'

Often shortened to 'hearts', this piece of Cockney rhyming slang can be dated to the nineteenth century.

hedge and ditch = market pitch

'I've got a nice hedge down in Covent Garden.'

As most nineteenth-century Cockneys would have had dealings with a market of some description or other, it is inevitable that a piece of slang was invented for the pitch on which the stalls stood.

hey-diddle-diddle = fiddle (violin)

'Play us a jig on the hey-diddle-diddle.'

Obviously this piece of slang is taken from the popular children's nursery rhyme 'Hey! Diddle, diddle! The cat and the fiddle'.

high-stepper = pepper

'Pass the high-stepper would you, son?'

Coined during World War I, the term 'high-stepper' is said to have referred to dancing girls.

Holy Friar = liar

'He is such a Friar!'

A term coined to mean a harmless liar as opposed to one involved in serious fraud.

horse and cart = heart/fart

'Have a horse and cart.'

Probably coined in the late nineteenth century, this phrase is often shortened to 'horse'. Also sometimes refers to the game of darts.

hot cross bun = gun

'Put down the hot cross bun and don't be rash.'

An innocuous-sounding term for a deadly weapon.

hot dinner = winner

'That chap's always a hot dinner.'

According to several sources this rhyme was coined because someone who won at the racetrack could afford an expensive, hot meal.

I

I desire = fire

'Put some more coals on the I desire.'

Not frequently used these days 'I desire' was coined in the Victorian period when nearly every household enjoyed a fireplace.

Irish jig = wig

'That's blatantly an Irish she's wearing.'

Variants for 'wig' include 'farmer's pig' and 'oil rig'.

iron tank = bank

'I need to get some money from the old iron.'

This is a great piece of rhyming slang in that it sums up perfectly the supposed security lent by a bank. A less common variant is 'tin tank'.

Isle of Wight = right (side)
'That pub on the Isle of Wight.'
One of the later pieces of Cockney this phrase was probably coined in the early twentieth century.

ivory pearl = girl
'She was a beautiful ivory.'
Although now almost obsolete this phrase is perhaps one of the prettier pieces of Cockney slang to have been invented.

Jack and Jill = hill/bill
'You've got to climb the old Jack and Jill.'
No doubt from the famous nursery rhyme 'Jack and Jill Went Up the Hill, occasionally this term can also mean a household bill.

Jack Jones = alone

'All on your Jack Jones, are you?'

Still very much in use today, this phrase probably originates in the late-nineteenth century. Sometimes shortened to Jack, i.e. 'She was all on her Jack in the corner.'

Jack Tar = bar

'We're off down the Jack Tar.'

A term most commonly used amongst theatre people. Jack Tar is a name for a sailor.

Jack the Ripper = kipper

'I fancy a nice Jack the Ripper.'

This phrase was coined in the late nineteenth century and refers to the way a kipper is normally served, i.e. with its stomach cut open.

Jamaica rum = thumb

'There's a splinter in me Jamaica.'

Given the amount Cockneys were used to drinking in the good old days, it is little wonder that so many pieces of slang refer to alcohol.

jam jar (also see la-di-dah) = car

'Get in the jam jar, we're off to the seaside.'

In its original context a 'jam jar' would have referred to a tramcar but as the motor car became an increasingly common sight on London's roads this particular piece of rhyming slang transferred beautifully to modern use.

jam tart = heart
'Me jam tart's beating so fast.'
As well as this phrase, Cockneys also refer to the 'heart' as 'raspberry tart' or 'strawberry tart'.

Jay Kay = a takeaway.
'Let's order a Jay Kay on the way home.'
Named after the British singer who became popular in the 1990s, having a 'Jay Kay' is a frequently used phrase for any type of takeaway from an Indian to fish and chips.

Jenny Linder = window
'Open the Jenny Linder.'
In order for this rhyme to work it is necessary to pronounce 'window' as 'winder'. A reference to the singer Jenny Lind, the 'Swedish nightingale'.

Jim Skinner = dinner
'Why's me Jim Skinner not on the table?'
As well as the popular 'Lilley & Skinner', this phrase is still used, as is 'saint and sinner'.

Jimmy Choo = shoe

'I can't find me other Jimmy Choo!'

Named after the famous shoe designer, a 'Jimmy Choo' can nowadays refer to any shoe in your wardrobe, not just the very expensive ones.

Joanna = piano

'Let's have a go on the old Joanna.'

As with the above 'Jenny Linder' in order for this rhyme to work the word 'piano' must be pronounced 'pianner'. In the nineteenth century singing around the piano was a popular entertainment for friends and family.

Joe Brown = town

'Which Joe Brown are we in this week?'

According to one source the phrase 'Joe Brown' was first coined by circus people in the mid-nineteenth century. Sometimes the phrase was changed to 'Mother Brown', although who these Browns were remains a mystery.

Joe Rourke = fork (pickpocket)

'Watch out, there are plenty of Joe Rourkes around here.'

In the eighteenth and nineteenth centuries a pickpocket was often referred to as a 'fork' (probably from their use of their fingers), hence this piece of rhyming slang.

Johnnie Horner = corner

'We'll meet at the Johnnie.'

Generally speaking this phrase is normally shortened to a 'Johnnie' – referring to a street corner as opposed to the corner of an object.

Johnnie Rutter = butter

'Pass the Johnnie Rutter, there's a luv.'

Mid-nineteenth century in origin – this phrase is often used simply to refer to bread and butter.

Judy and Punch = lunch

'What's for Judy and Punch?'

An inversion of the popular Punch and Judy, this piece of rhyming slang, alongside 'kidney punch' is a popular phrase.

Kate and Sydney = steak and kidney

'We're having a lovely Kate and Sydney for tea tonight.'

A once hugely popular British dish, this rhyme was probably dreamt up because 'Sydney' is one of the few words that rhymes with 'kidney'.

'Beefsteak pudding? Phew! A pity Johnny's not here, Ma!

Remember how he used to go for your Kate and Sidney?'

Marguerite Steen, 1949

Kate Carney = army

'Watch out, the Kate Carney's round the corner!'

Referring to the popular music-hall artiste, this phrase was coined during World War I presumably because many of the troops enjoyed listening to the songstress.

Kate Moss = toss

'I couldn't give a Kate.'

A recent addition to Cockney rhyming slang, this phrase was most probably coined not because supermodel Kate Moss doesn't 'give a toss' but because her name fits the rhyme beautifully.

King Lear = ear

'God, my King Lears don't half hurt.'

Used predominantly amongst theatrical folk (after the Shakespeare play of that name) the phrase is thought to have originated in the early part of the twentieth century.

kings and queens = beans

'Do you want kings and queens with your toast?'

Most often referring to baked beans, nonetheless this phrase can be used to describe green beans, runner beans, etc.

knife and fork = pork

'Go to the market and get me some knife and fork.'

This is the longest-serving rhyme for 'pork'; 'Duchess of York' is a more recent addition and refers to Prince Andrew's ex-wife Sarah Ferguson who had a very public battle to lose weight.

ℒ

la-di-dah (also see jam jar) = car
'Look at her in her new la-di-dah.'
A relatively recent addition to the Cockney rhyming slang lexicon – the term 'la-di-dah' is thought to be a disparaging remark referring as much to someone's jealousy at their neighbour's new vehicle as to the vehicle itself!

Lady Godiva = fiver (i.e. five-pound note)
'She only had a Lady in her pocket.'
At one point this phrase almost became obsolete but in recent years 'Lady Godiva' has seen a revival.

lean and fat = hat
'Best put your lean on before you go out.'
A nineteenth-century term coined when hats were more widely worn on a daily basis.

Lilley & Skinner = dinner
'Where's my Lilley & Skinner?'
This phrase refers to the famous shoe shop Lilley & Skinner, which was founded in 1835 and is still going strong.

Lillian Gish = fish
'We're having Lillian for dinner.'
A none-too-flattering rhyme given that Lillian Gish, star of the silver screen, was a renowned beauty in her day.

linen draper = paper (i.e. newspaper)
'I'm going down the shops for a linen.'
Normally shortened to 'linen', according to Julian Franklyn in his seminal work, *A Dictionary of Rhyming Slang*, the phrase applies particularly to newspapers rather than paper in general.

Little Nell = bell
'That Little Nell's been ringing since dawn.'
Named after Dickens's creation, Little Nell from *The Old Curiosity Shop* (1841) whose maudlin deathbed scene has become the butt of many jokes – 'Little Nell' also has connotations of the knell heard at a funeral.

Little Tich = itch
'I've got a Little Tich and it's driving me mad!'
This piece of slang comes from the name of the comedian Harry Relph whose nickname was 'Little Tich' because he was so short.

loaf of bread = head
'For godsakes use your loaf.'
Nowadays the term 'loaf' is commonly used to mean 'head', but this piece of slang was originally coined in the nineteenth century and often referred to the process of 'thinking' rather than the actual head itself. A less common variant is 'twopenny loaf'.

Londonderry = sherry
'Pour a Londonderry for your old mother.'
Londonderry is a city in Northern Ireland, although not one that is particularly renowned for sherry-drinking!

Lord Lovell = shovel
'Get started on that hole with your Lord Lovell.'
Often used on board a ship, Lord Lovell was first recorded circa 1857.

lord mayor = swear
'Don't you lord mayor, or else!'
Used exclusively in a profane sense as opposed to a judicial one, 'lord mayoring' is a very popular phrase.

Lord Wigg = pig
'She's as fat as a Lord Wigg.'
Not a very flattering allusion to the Labour politician Lord George Wigg (1900-1983).

Lucy Locket = pocket

'What've you got in your Lucy?'

Taken from the famous nursery rhyme, 'Lucy Locket lost her pocket, Kitty Fisher found it', this phrase originates in the Victorian period and still enjoys some currency today. 'Sky rocket' is a less popular variant.

macaroni = pony (i.e. £25)

'That's a macaroni you owe me.'

First used by bookmakers, the term pony is a piece of slang in itself, so one could describe 'macaroni' as a piece of double-slang!

maids adorning = morning

'It's too early in the maids.'

Frequently shortened to 'maids' this phrase probably refers to the early hour at which maidservants had to rise in order to clean the house, set new fires, and prepare for breakfast.

man and wife = a knife (pocket knife)
'Put that man and wife down.'
Almost obsolete these days this phrase was very popular during World
War I when most soldiers would carry penknives of some description.

Mars Bar = a scar
'Look at the mars on that face!'
Although the Mars Bar – a chocolate and toffee confectionary – was first
registered in 1932, the rhyme 'Mars Bar' meaning a scar isn't thought to
have been used in Cockney rhyming slang until the 1970s.

meat pie = fly
'That stench is attracting the meat pies.'
A none-too-savoury piece of slang that rather puts you off your food.
Another phrase for 'fly' is a 'Nellie Bligh'.

Melvyn Bragg = shag
'I'm only interested in a Melvyn.'
One doubts whether the writer and broadcaster, Melvyn Bragg, would be
too pleased that his name is used to mean having sex; nonetheless this is a
very popular phrase.

Michael Caine = pain
'He's a right Michael Caine.'

Given the actor Michael Caine's Cockney roots, it seems only fitting that his name should be included in the lexicon of rhyming slang.

Mickey Mouse = a house
'That's a fine Mickey you've just bought.'
In its earliest form 'Mickey Mouse' meaning 'house' was normally used to describe a theatrical audience i.e. 'It's a full Mickey tonight.' However, latterly the phrase also refers to a residential property. See also 'cat and mouse'.

mince pies = eyes
'What a lovely pair of minces.'
Still in evidence today, this piece of Cockney rhyming slang was first recorded in the mid-nineteenth century when it enjoyed huge popularity.

monkey's tails = nails
'Pass the monkey's, will you?'
Most often used amongst Cockney carpenters, this phrase is still current.

Mother Hubbard = cupboard
'Go to the Mother, dear, and fetch me some flour.'
Taking its lead from the popular nursery rhyme 'Old Mother Hubbard, She went to the cupboard,' this phrase is often shortened to 'mother' and can still be heard today.

Mother Kelly = jelly

'Do you want some Mother Kelly with that?'

Taking its inspiration from the old music-hall song 'On Mother Kelly's Doorstep', this refers to both sweet and savoury jelly.

mother's ruin = gin

'Give us a drop of mother's ruin.'

Not the best piece of rhyming slang seeing as 'ruin' doesn't really rhyme with 'gin', nonetheless this was and still is a popular phrase describing as it does what happens when you drink too much of the stuff!

Mrs Duckett = bucket

'Get some cod out the Mrs Duckett, quick as you like.'

Most commonly used amongst fishmongers who keep fish in huge buckets of water and/or ice; this has its origins in the Victorian period.

Mutt and Jeff = deaf

'God, he's Mutt and Jeff.'

Based on comic-strip characters created in the 1930s, this piece of slang can still be heard on the streets of London.

Myleene Klass = arse

'Have you seen the Myleene on that!'

Doubtless the singer and TV presenter Myleene Klass wouldn't be too impressed that her name had entered the Cockney lexicon with reference to the human bottom, but given that Ms Klass's name is pronounced to rhyme so perfectly with arse, the pairing was somewhat inevitable.

nanny goat = boat
'Let's hire a nanny and go out on the lake.'
Not quite as popular as 'frog in the throat' or 'hat and coat', nonetheless 'nanny goat', which was in use during the 1940s, can still be heard today.

near and far = bar
'We're off down the near and far.'
Derived from the popular phrase 'so near, and yet so far' this slang for a bar or pub is rooted in the early part of the twentieth century, when going to the pub of an evening was a way of life for most working men.

needle and pin = gin

'I'm going down the pub for a needle.'

There are several phrases in Cockney for 'gin', including 'Vera Lynn' and 'Lincoln's Inn', but 'needle and pin' is probably the most popular.

Nelly Duff = puff (i.e. life)

'Not on your nelly!'

Whether or not there was an original Nelly Duff is unknown, but the phrase 'not on your nelly' meaning 'certainly not' or 'unlikely' has now spread far wider than Cockney rhyming slang to become common parlance. Coined in the 1940s, the term 'Nelly Duff' was also used to rhyme with 'poof', i.e. homosexual.

Noah's ark = nark (informant)

'Watch out for him, he's a Noah.'

Criminal activity ran rife in London's East End during the Victorian period hence the fact that there are several words for 'informants' (see also 'grasshopper.') A 'Noah' was not a popular person.

north and south = mouth

'Watch your north and south, luv.'

Early nineteenth century in origin, this is one of the oldest surviving pieces of Cockney rhyming slang.

nose and chin = win

'I've had a nose on the horses.'

Frequently used in bookmaking circles, this early-twentieth-century piece of slang was probably coined to describe the fact that a winning horse would be a nose and a chin in front of its rivals.

nosey my knacker = tobacco

'Where've you put me nosey?'

This curious rhyme was first recorded in the nineteenth century and appears in Henry Mayhew's highly regarded work *London Labour and the London Poor* (1851).

nuclear sub = pub

'I'm off down the nuclear.'

This relatively modern phrase for every Londoner's favourite place is an example of how Cockney rhyming slang is constantly evolving.

oak and ash = cash
'Have you any oak on you?'
Normally confined to the theatrical fraternity, 'oak and ash' is a good example of early-twentieth-century slang. See also 'sausage and mash'.

oily rag = fag (cigarette)
'Give us an oily.'
Usually employed by manual workers and apt because the white cigarette paper would become dirty when handled by these men and women, the phrase 'oily rag' is thought to have originated in the early twentieth century.

old pot and pan = old man (husband)
'Listen to the old pot, he's your elder.'
Dating from the nineteenth century 'old pot and pan' usually refers to the father of the family, i.e. the old pot!

Oliver Twist = fist
'Put your Olivers down and let's have a drink.'
Named after the Charles Dickens novel, *Oliver Twist* – to use one's 'Olivers'

was popular slang in the mid-nineteenth century and still enjoys some currency today.

on the floor = poor
'She's on the floor.'
This piece of rhyming slang from the nineteenth century sums up perfectly the state of being penniless.

orchestra stalls = balls
'He's not got the orchestras!'
Nearly always shortened to 'orchestras'. Coincidentally, 'orchi' is the Greek root for testicles, as in 'orchiectomy'.

Oxford scholar = dollar
'He's plenty of Oxfords.'
Said to have been coined in the West of England, this phrase is normally shortened to 'Oxford', as the following quote illustrates.

> 'We'll say a quid deposit, returnable on return of the hat, and a straight charge of an Oxford for the loan. Right.'
>
> Anthony Burgess, *The Doctor is Sick* (1960)

Pat and Mike = a bike
'I've a brand new Pat and Mike.'
A nineteenth-century phrase for a commonly used mode of transport.

peas in the pot = hot
'Blimey, she's peas!'
Not usually referring to the weather, this phrase more commonly describes
how attractive a girl is!

pen and ink = a stink
'What a pen and ink!'
A very popular mid-nineteenth-century piece of Cockney, 'pen and ink'
was made famous when the TV series *Minder* was first aired in Britain.
    'That old cigar don't half pen and ink, don't it?'
                                                    Barry Purchase, *Minder* (1983)

Pete Tong = wrong
'It's all gone a bit Pete Tong.'
Named after the British disc jockey, Pete Tong, this very popular phrase is
still widely used today.

Peter Pan = van

'Get the tools out the back of me Peter.'

Named after the eponymous hero of J. M. Barrie's play and novels, this early-nineteenth-century piece of rhyming slang is still current, although sometimes replaced with 'pot and pan'.

pimple and blotch = Scotch (whisky)

'Do you fancy a pimple?'

No doubt referring to the effect on the skin of drinking too much whisky, 'pimple and blotch' arrived on the scene in the early twentieth century.

pipe your eye = cry

'Stop your piping.'

Still current today this piece of Cockney was very popular from the mid-nineteen hundreds onwards.

pitch and toss = boss

'Go ask the pitch and toss.'

One of the later pieces of rhyming slang, this phrase was coined in the 1940s after a game which involved pitching or tossing coins into the air and is used mostly amongst theatrical folk.

plates of meat = feet
'God, me plates are aching!'
A very popular piece of slang this phrase can still be heard on the streets of London, particularly amongst hard-nosed shoppers!

pleasure and pain = rain
'I wish this pleasure and pain would stop.'
Not the oldest piece of Cockney rhyming slang but one of the most descriptive given that farmers often need rain for their crops to grow but not so much that the harvest is ruined.

pork pie = lie
'Stop telling porkies!'
Coined in the 1970s, this popular phrase in no way implies that pigs are mendacious! Often the phrase is changed to 'porky pie' or 'porkies'.

potatoes in the mould = cold
'Cor it's 'taters today!'
Coined in the nineteenth century but usually shortened to ''taters,' no doubt this phrase owes its origins to the fact that in very cold weather potatoes freeze in the ground.

Q

Quaker Oat = coat
'It's cold out there, you'll need your quaker.'
The breakfast cereal company of the same name was founded in the 1870s, so there's a good chance that this slang dates back a long way.

**Queen's Park Rangers
(also see 'Glasgow Rangers')** = strangers
'The pub's full of Queen's Park Rangers.'
As with the phrase 'Glasgow Rangers' the phrase 'Queen's Park Rangers' is the name of a British football club, only this one is based in west London, not Scotland. Cockney includes a lot of words for 'strangers', probably because it was originally created by ne'er-do-wells who were always on the look out for police or informants.

Quentin Tarantino = wine (vino)
'Pour us a glass of Quentin, will you?'
Named after the Hollywood director of films such as *Reservoir Dogs* and *Pulp Fiction* – Quentin Tarantino gives a contemporary rhyme for an age old drink.

R

rabbit and pork = talk
'Will you stop rabbitting!'
One of the ten most popular Cockney phrases 'rabbit and pork' is usually
shortened to 'rabbit' meaning 'incessant chatter' and was immortalized in
the 1980 song 'Rabbit' by Chas & Dave.

Radio Ones = runs (i.e. diarrhoea)
'Christ, I've got the Radios.'
Coined in the twentieth century to describe yet another embarrassing
complaint.

read and write = fight
'Stop that read and writing.'
Mid-nineteenth century in origin – a 'reader and writer' means a 'fighter.'

Richard the Third = bird
'Does that Richard fly?'
Generally believed to be used mostly within theatrical circles after the
Shakespeare play, this piece of slang describes birds of the feathered variety
– usually pigeons and sparrows – both species being connected to London.

rip and tear = swear

'Don't you rip and tear.'

Another very apt piece of slang describing the sharpness of tongue required when swearing at or cursing someone. 'To rip someone apart' is a figurative expression, which stems from the Cockney.

Rory O'Moore = door

'Shut the Rory, will you?'

Originally a 'Rory O'Moore' referred to a 'floor' but at some point in the nineteenth century the phrase changed to mean 'door'. Rory O'Moore was an Irish rebel immortalized in song and book.

Rosie Lee/Rosy Lea = tea

'Let's have a nice cup of Rosie Lee.'

A classic piece of Cockney rhyming slang, the first recorded use of this phrase is from 1920. 'Nanny Lee' is a less common variant.

rub-a-dub = a pub/club

'I'm off down the rub.'

Taken no doubt from the nursery rhyme 'Rub-a-dub-dub' but usually shortened to 'rub'.

Ruby Rose = nose
'Look at the Ruby on him!'
Obviously referring to someone who enjoys their alcohol (hence their red nose), 'Ruby Rose' and 'Irish Rose' were once both popular rhymes.

salmon and trout = stout (beer)
'I couldn't half do with a salmon.'
With its roots firmly planted in the nineteenth century, this piece of rhyming slang is one of the oldest and most sustained.

satin and silk = milk
'Go and get a pint of satin, would you.'
A smooth evocation of this foodstuff, 'satin and silk' has replaced the nineteenth-century phrase 'yellow silk'.

saucepan lid = quid (or occasionally 'kid')
'Lend us a saucepan.'
Late nineteenth century in origin but still enjoying some currency today.

sausage and mash = cash/crash

'Can you lend me some sausage, Mum?'

A good wholesome meal – no wonder 'sausage and mash' is rhyming slang for cash. It can also be used to mean a 'crash', as in a car accident. Also see 'oak and ash'.

Scapa Flow = go

'Where's he Scapa'd to?'

Coined after World War I, 'Scapa Flow' usually refers to someone going *from* somewhere (often in a hurry). Commonly thought to be the origin of the word 'to scarper' meaning 'to escape'.

Scotch eggs = legs

'Blimey, did you see the Scotches on her?'

Dating from the nineteen hundreds there are several variations on the word 'eggs' meaning 'legs', i.e. 'fried eggs', 'bacon and eggs' and 'scrambled eggs', on top of which the phrase 'Scotch pegs' is also commonly used.

septic tank = Yank (American)

'Don't mind him, he's a septic.'

There are several other phrases used for 'Yank', of which this is the most popular, including 'ham shank', 'Sherman tank' and 'wooden plank'.

Sexton Blake = cake
'Let's have a nice slice of Sexton Blake.'
Sexton Blake – the famous detective who thrilled readers in the early twentieth century, much as Sherlock Holmes had done in the nineteenth – is at the root of this rhyming slang for 'cake'.

silver spoon = moon
'There's a full silver tonight.'
A very apt description for a thing of beauty, 'silver spoon', or 'silver' as it's usually shortened to, dates from the late twentieth century.

Sinbad the sailor = tailor
'I'm off to the Sinbad to get me suit.'
Mid-twentieth century in origin.

Sir Walter Scott = pot (of beer)
'Get us a couple of Walters in, barmaid.'
Taken from the name of the author of *Ivanhoe* and *The Heart of Midlothian*, among other novels, this phrase doesn't refer to cooking equipment but the jars that beer used to be served in.

sit-down-beside-her = spider
'Watch the sit-down-beside-her!'
Taken from the popular children's nursery rhyme, 'Little Miss Muffet', this is

also said to have been inspired by the fact that outside toilets often housed large spiders which scared anyone who went in to use the facilities!

skin and blister = sister
'She's my skin and blister.'
Dating from the nineteenth century this phrase is seldom shortened.

sorry and sad = bad
'That's so sorry and sad!'
Not the most frequently used piece of slang, nevertheless it is still occasionally heard today.

stand at ease = fleas (or occasionally 'cheese')
'That dog's covered in stands.'
Originating during World War I when fleas were rife among the serving forces – particularly those confined to the trenches – this phrase can still be heard today.

steam tug = mug (fool)
'I feel like such a steamer.'
Coined in the nineteenth century and frequently shortened. Other phrases for a 'mug' include 'hearthrug' and the less common 'Tom Tug'.

stewed prune = tune

'Give us a stewed on the old Joanna.'

Every Cockney enjoys a good singsong around the piano, so it is inevitable that there should be a rhyme for a tune.

T

take and give = live

'I want to take and give forever.'

Nineteenth century in origin, this inversion of the usual 'give and take' perhaps refers to the advice given to couples in order that they might live out a happy marriage.

tea leaf = thief

'He's nothing but a tea leaf.'

Why this particular piece of Cockney rhyming slang is still so popular is anybody's guess, but having been recorded by C. Charles Booth in his book *Life and Labour of the People of London*, 'tea leaf' is still amongst the top ten pieces of nineteenth-century slang used today.

teapot lid = quid (one pound)
'Give us a teapot for the quiz machine.'
Sometimes referred to as a 'saucepan lid', this piece of Cockney for a 'quid' is often shortened simply to 'teapot'.

tiddly wink = a drink
'Let's have a tiddly wink.'
Generally believed to have first appeared in *Punch* magazine circa 1895, being a little tiddly (meaning 'drunk') is one of the oldest and yet most commonly used pieces of rhyming slang current today.

Tom and Dick = sick
'I'm feeling a bit Tom and Dick.'
Variants include 'Moby Dick' and occasionally 'Uncle Dick'. Having a 'dicky tummy' stems from this phrase.

tomfoolery = jewellery
'She's got a huge box of tomfoolery in her bedroom.'
Coined in the early part of the twentieth century – the shortened form 'tom' is even more popular these days within criminal circles.

Tommy Tucker = supper

'Let's sit down for our Tommy.'

Nineteenth century in origin, this expression comes from the popular nursery rhyme 'Little Tommy Tucker', who sang 'for his supper'.

Tom Thumb = rum

'Give me a drop of Tom Thumb.'

Most popular amongst sailors who traditionally like a drop of rum to keep them warm on cold nights.

trouble and strife = wife

'Got to get home to the old trouble and strife!'

A misogynistic phrase that is supposedly meant to be humorous, this piece of Cockney rhyming slang is still in frequent use today.

turtle doves = gloves

'Better put your turtles on.'

Nineteenth century in origin 'turtle doves' is a lot less frequently used than in Victorian times when every lady owned at least one pair.

Uncle Ned = bed
'That's a very comfortable Uncle Ned.'
Uncle Ned is perhaps the most popular phrase for 'a bed' in the lexicon of Cockney rhyming slang although who Uncle Ned was has never been discovered!

Uncle Sam = lamb
'We're having Uncle Sam for lunch.'
Not frequently used today but nonetheless still current.

Uncle Willy = silly
'God, he was Uncle Willy!'
Very popular in the early twentieth century, this phrase is also frequently used to describe someone who is simple-minded or childish.

Uri Geller = Stella (beer)
'I'll have a pint of Uri please, love.'
Using the name of the spoon-bending psychic, this piece of modern slang is often heard today.

Vera Lynn = gin
'Two Veras please, barman.'
Coined in the mid-twentieth century and still current amongst the theatrical fraternity, this phrase is taken from the name of the famous singer and actress.

Vincent Price = ice
'I'll have a bit of Vincent in that whisky.'
Another famous screen legend lends his name to this phrase, still in use today.

Wallace and Gromit = vomit
'Watch out, he's about to Wallace and Gromit.'
Named after the much-loved plasticine film characters created by Nick Park, this is a very popular phrase for being sick.

weasel and stoat = coat
'Get your weasel, we're going out.'
Normally shortened, this is the most popular rhyme for a 'coat', although 'Quaker oat' and 'nanny goat' are still occasionally heard.

weeping willow = pillow

'I cried into my weeping willow all night.'

According to Ayto, this phrase was first recorded in 1880 and is still current today.

whistle and flute = a suit

'That's a fine whistle you're wearing, sir.'

A very popular phrase, often shortened to 'whistle'. A less common variant is 'piccolo and flute', not to be confused with 'piccolos and flutes' meaning 'boots'.

William Hill = pill

'Where are my William Hills?'

According to several sources this piece of rhyming slang was coined in the 1990s and is named after the chain of bookmakers, William Hill – branches of which appear on nearly every High Street in the country.

X, Y, Z

you and me = tea

A less popular term than 'Rosie Lee' nonetheless 'you and me' is still used.

ENGLISH TO COCKNEY

advice Anneka Rice
alone Jack Jones
army Kate Carney
arse Myleene Klass
aunt garden plant

B

bad sorry and sad
balls Davina McCalls, orchestra stalls
banana Gertie Gitana
bank iron tank, tin tank
bar Jack Tar, near and far
barrow cock sparrow
beans kings and queens
bed Uncle Ned
beers Britney Spears
believe Adam and Eve
bell Little Nell
belly Auntie Nellie

bill Jack and Jill
bike Pat and Mike
bird Richard the Third
bitter (beer) apple fritter, giggle and titter
boat frog in the throat, hat and coat, nanny goat
boil Conan Doyle
book Captain Cook
boots daisy roots
boss pitch and toss
bottle Aristotle
braces airs and graces
brandy fine and dandy, Mahatma Gandhi
breasts (tits) Brad Pitts
broke (penniless) hearts of oak
bucket Mrs Duckett
bum fife and drum
butter Dan Tucker, Johnnie Rutter

cake give and take, Sexton Blake
candle Harry Randall
car jam jar, la-di-dah
cash oak and ash, sausage and mash
cat ball of fat, this and that
cell flowery dell
cheque goose's neck
chicken Charlie Dicken
cigarette (fag) oily rag
clock dickory dock
coach cockroach
coat Quaker Oat, weasel and stoat
cold potatoes in the mould
copper (policeman) grasshopper
corner Johnnie Horner
crash sausage and mash
crook babbling brook
cry pipe your eye
cupboard Mother Hubbard

D, E

deaf Mutt and Jeff
diarrhoea (runs) Radio Runs
dinner Jim Skinner, Lilley & Skinner
dog cherry hog
dole (the labour (exchange)) beggar-my-neighbour
dollar Oxford scholar
door Rory O'Moore
drink tiddly-wink
dripping Doctor Crippen
drunk elephant's trunk
ear King Lear
egg borrow and beg
eyes mince pies

F

face Boat Race
fart horse and cart
feet plates of meat
fiddle (violin) hey-diddle-diddle

fight read and write
fine Calvin Klein
fire Anna Maria, Ave Maria, I desire
first (degree) Geoff Hurst
fish Lillian Gish
fist Oliver Twist
fiver Lady Godiva
fleas stand at ease
flowers early hours
fly meat pie

gay Doris Day
gin mother's ruin, needle and pin, Vera Lynn
girl ivory pearl
gloves turtle doves
go Scapa Flow
gravy army and navy
greens (vegetables) has beens
gun hot cross bun
gutter bread and butter

H

haddock Bessie Braddock
haemorrhoids (piles) Chalfont St Giles, Farmer Giles,
Nuremberg Trials

hair Barnet Fair
handle Harry Randall
hat lean and fat
head loaf of bread
heart horse and cart, jam tart, raspberry/strawberry tart
hill Jack and Jill
hot (attractive) peas in the pot
house cat and mouse, Mickey Mouse, rat and mouse

I & J

ice Vincent Price
itch Little Tich
jail bucket and pail
jelly Mother Kelly
jewellery tomfoolery
judge Barnaby Rudge

K

kettle Hansel and Gretel
kids dustbin lids, God forbids, saucepan lids
kipper Jack the Ripper
knackered (tired) cream crackered
knees biscuits and cheese
knickers (undies) Eddie Grundies
knife (all) drum and fife
knife (pocket) man and wife

L

lamb Uncle Sam
lark (i.e. a joke) Bushey Park
laugh bubble bath, giraffe, Steffi Graf
legs bacon and eggs, fried eggs, Scotch eggs
liar Holy Friar
lie pork pie
life (puff) Nelly Duff
lips apple pips, battleships
live take and give

liver cheerful giver
lodger artful dodger
look butcher's hook
lunch Judy and Punch, kidney punch

magistrate garden gate
market pitch hedge and ditch
married cut and carried
matches cuts and scratches
mate china plate
milk satin and silk, yellow silk
minute cock linnet
moon silver spoon
money bread and honey
mouth north and south
morning maids adorning
mug (fool) steam tug
mutton Billy Button

N, O

nails monkeys' tails
nark (informant) Noah's ark
neck bushel and peck, Gregory Peck
night black and white, take a fright
nose Ruby Rose
old man old pot and pan
onions corns and bunions

P

pain Michael Caine
pants fleas and ants
paper (newspaper) linen draper
penniless (broke) hearts of oak
penny Abergavenny
pepper high-stepper
phone dog and bone
piano Joanna
pickles Harvey Nichols
pickpocket (fork) Joe Rourke

pig Lord Wigg
pill William Hill
pillow weeping willow
pinch (steal) half-inch
pipe cherry ripe
play night and day
pocket Lucy Locket, sky rocket
pony (£25) macaroni
poor on the floor
pork knife and fork
pot (i.e. a pot of beer) Sir Walter Scott
pox (syphilis) band in the box
prostitute (whore) bolt the door, boat and oar, Jane Shore
pub nuclear sub, rub-a-dub

queer (homosexual) ginger beer
quid saucepan lid, teapot lid
races (i.e. horseraces) belt and braces
rain pleasure and pain
rat bowler hat

rent Burton-on-Trent
right (side) Isle of Wight
road frog and toad
Rolls-Royce Camilla Parker Bowles
row bull and cow
rum Tom Thumb

saw (tool) bear's paw
scar Mars Bar
Scotch (whisky) pimple and blotch
Scouts Brussels sprouts
sense eighteen pence
shag Melvyn Bragg
shave dig a grave
sheep Bo Peep
sherry Londonderry
ship halfpenny dip
shirt Dicky Dirt
shoe Jimmy Choo
shovel Lord Lovell

sick Tom and Dick
silly daffadown dilly, Uncle Willy
sister skin and blister
sleep Bo Peep
socks almond rocks
son (also sun) currant bun
song ding-dong
soup bowl the hoop
sparrow bow and arrow
spider sit-down-beside-her
stairs apples and pears
steak Ben Flake
steak and kidney Kate and Sydney
steal (pinch) half-inch
Stella (beer) Uri Geller
stink pen and ink
stout (beer) salmon and trout
strangers Glasgow Rangers, Queen's Park Rangers
street field of wheat
suit piccolo and flute, whistle and flute
supper Tommy Tucker
swear lord mayor, rip and tear

T

table Cain and Abel
tailor Sinbad the Sailor
takeaway Jay Kay
tale Daily Mail
talk rabbit and pork
tea Rosie Lee, Rosy Lea, Nanny Lee, you and me
teeth Bexleyheath, Hampstead Heath
ticket bat and wicket
time birdlime
thief tea leaf
thumb Jamaica rum
tobacco nosey my knacker
toe stop and go
tongue brewer's bung
tools April fools
toss Kate Moss
town Joe Brown, Mother Brown
tripe (nonsense) cherry ripe
trouble Barney Rubble
trousers round the houses
tune stewed prune

turkey bubbly jock

umbrella Auntie Ella, Isabella
understand (twig) earwig
undies (underwear) Eddie Grundies
van Peter Pan, pot and pan
vomit Wallace and Gromit

wages greengages
walk ball of chalk
wash Bob Squash
water fisherman's daughter
whisky gay and frisky
whore bolt the door, boat and oar, Jane Shore
wife carving knife, trouble and strife
wig farmer's pig, Irish jig, oil rig

win nose and chin
wine (vino) Quentin Tarantino
window Jenny Linder
winner hot dinner
word dicky bird
wrong Pete Tong

X, Y, Z

Yank ham shank, septic tank, Sherman tank, wooden plank

BIBLIOGRAPHY

Ayto, John, *Oxford Dictionary of Rhyming Slang*, Oxford University Press, Oxford 2003

Franklyn, Julian; *A Dictionary of Rhyming Slang*, Routledge & Kegan Paul, London 1961

Jones, Jack, *Rhyming Cockney Slang*, Abson Books, Bristol 1973

Lewin, Esther and Lewin, Albert, *The Wordsworth Thesaurus of Slang*, Wordsworth Editions, Herts, 1995

Orwell, George, *Down and Out in Paris and London*, Penguin Books, 1945

For more great books see
www.mombooks.com